USED WITH PERMISSION

# Used with Permission

Charlie Pendergast

*San Francisco, California*

© 2020 Charlie Pendergast

All rights reserved

ISBN-13: 978-1-7329439-7-1

"A Yearning to Wrinkle" was first published in the New York Times Magazine, November 22, 2020; and "Shuddering in Place" was first published in the verse anthology *Stay Inspired: Shelter in Place 2020* (San Francisco: Dolby Chadwick Gallery, 2020).

The author wishes to thank Lisa Chadwick for her friendship and enthusiastic support; Alex Kanevsky for graciously allowing us to his painting for the cover; and Michael Christianson for reading the manuscript and offering his thoughts and useful corrections.

Cover artwork by Alex Kanevsky

Author photo by Kevin Conner

*San Francisco, California*

for:

*the precious ones
I overthrew for an
education in the world*
—*Leonard Cohen*

and, as always, to Kevin Connor

# CONTENTS

*Preface*     1

| | |
|---|---|
| Pages | 3 |
| Chariness in Doubt | 4 |
| Waiting Rooms | 5 |
| Portents | 6 |
| Duties Relieved | 7 |
| The Choice | 8 |
| Agog in Banter | 9 |
| The Gamble | 10 |
| The Skin of our Seeking | 11 |
| The Villainy of Success | 12 |
| The Haunt of Depression | 13 |
| Relics | 14 |
| Defeat | 15 |
| The Brink | 16 |
| Wine on the Deck | 17 |
| Finish What? | 18 |
| Spawn of Barnum | 19 |
| Her Child | 20 |
| To Postpone | 21 |
| Gaps | 22 |
| Default | 23 |
| Shuddering in Place | 24 |
| A Yearning to Wrinkle | 25 |
| Blantons or Knob Creek | 26 |
| Unknown Others | 28 |
| Guess Again | 29 |
| A Deathbed | 30 |
| Old Friends | 31 |
| A Generous Sip | 32 |
| Shades Up | 33 |

| | |
|---|---|
| An Edit | 34 |
| Sweet Shards of Dark Cherries | 35 |
| Sheltering | 36 |
| Changing Stacks | 38 |
| Forts | 40 |
| A Taunt of Clues | 41 |
| A Gentle Death | 42 |
| An Obvious Reset | 43 |
| Ardor in Place | 44 |
| Summer Flies | 45 |
| For Now | 47 |
| The Drift | 49 |

# PREFACE

Poets are always newcomers, immigrants to every moment, so, if and how they settle, as outsiders, aliens, conformists, nativists, pranksters, criminals or priests, they are shy, usually awkward, hesitant to bring forth their work, and hesitant not to. *Used with Permission*, a phrase now made to do the work of a title, is meant to express a mood, or perhaps a style, of submission to the relentless condition of thinking; additionally, here in these pages it reflects the musings of our recent, sometimes difficult year.

A poem is a sudden moment, plying a barge of phrases along a channel, within sight of some nearby shore. Long or short, it is often noisy with tempered insights, pain, shame, the doleful news of duty, or, better, some hopeful, simple joys, or litanies of delight, that share in the visible or hidden beauty of being alive. Poems are also a pulsing salute to our instinctual incessant thinking. Most poets feel they have been sentenced to this for life, so after clawing their way into and out from random solitudes, they do their timorous reporting and beseeching from behind imaginary bars. Being now in your hands is to land far from an earlier, cozier home.

As with all I do that's called poetry, I've placed this here to be found later. To offer these poems as finished is to admit to a necessary lie. We who play and work in the multiple Edens of words, whose joy and anguish comes from deciphering magnitudes from dross or treasure, are never satisfied with what we push onto the so-called reality of a page. Lives spent in the service to this demand, the siren call of any urge to make art, is mostly motivated entirely by love; a love which annihilates all other bastard motivations, and which we've learned to tentatively trust during the long waiting in our lives.

It is not just the evoking of a mood, or an eloquent turn of phrase that unites (or rewrites) the ephemeral with the physical; it is not wind and brittle branches, or snow, or footprints. It is, more, the emerging of revelations that cascade; natural emissions of mind, impressions, linkages forming like overlapping tiles, to be opened and reviewed. Poetry is thinking that must halt, suddenly, in the fair, the just, disposition of a moment.

Charlie Pendergast<br>
Sebastopol, California

# PAGES

There is humanity in all our words,
yet, we remain unsatisfied,
persisting in needy agitation,
awaiting the next unique pleasure,
or the relief from too much data.
I do not drift in long voyages of loneliness,
but in acres of narcotic absence,
of distraction.
In hours alone,
doing only this,
this filling of pages
with the stuff of the moment,
not given to judgement,
or guilt,
but quietly listening
and patiently waiting
for the phrases to well up,
gaseous or rapturous,
nervous or glib or swift.
I give what is there to the page.
Not straining.
Merely reporting.

## CHARINESS IN DOUBT

They did not *teach* us respect.
They made us look at it,
focus on its might,
see the human need of it.
The men, the women,
their colors, all children,
their eyes, their yearning,
their need to know the truth of place,
the *where* where we each stand,
and how we shed the skins of our selves
on behalf of the world, together,
in the justice of mutual caretaking,
in the lives we contribute to our patch
of space, to our families,
communities, countries, the planet.
They showed us how to shape our mouths,
to use our words,
especially for each delicate moment
of listening,
where the pros and cons of action
meet a cosmic hesitancy.
The caustic lingo of judgement
is vanquished in the relief
of admitting to *not knowing*,
to trusting the goodliness of doubt.
They advised us to put a voice
in our poems that is not abstract,
that is not a new brand of mania,
or serves the mysteries of
competing cults.
They said say it, say it,
add your voice,
what do you bring that there
is time for?
They said be human revolvers,
speakers of useful harms.

# WAITING ROOMS

The morning, recently free from dreaming,
is a newly painted room, aching to be occupied,
into which we rehang our limited and tattered ambitions,
adjusting for the play of light,
admitting, reluctantly, again,
the double-edged curse of repetition.

We the people,
of our rooms, our homes, streets, neighborhoods,
cities, boroughs, counties, states, nations, continents:
embedded in a matrix, subdued, alas, by the powers of ten.
Hopeful, daily, that this new room,
surprising,
but not,
inspires the fortitude to continue.

Speak the words.
Tap the rhythm,
play the color,
if it feels right,
settle in.

## PORTENTS

The life within a moment,
leaps from heart to page
in minds
where phrases form as dew might
in the lower elevations of hope,
where great differences collide,
and some magic appears as sinking,
settling, shifting, veering hopes;
and the artists within the artists
do their hapless but vital discerning
and report,
word by word,
in pithy skirmishes of ideas,
the phrases that subdue chaos,
and draw near our hearts
manufacturing the radical heat of wishing,
that we all live to savor
and would gladly die for.

So, welcome too
the abbreviated smiling indictments
the balancing portents
that just in time,
potent with secrets,
whisper latent incantations
of needed blessings
or the daily curse of need.

## DUTIES RELIEVED

It is intimacy
that we invite into these bleak landscapes,
these testing grounds of integrity.
Will you endure?
Are you torn apart?
Are you reminded of when you smoked
and could wait and wait, anywhere,
as long as a cigarette could curl
thoughts and moments of drifting
above your head.
Are you made whole?

The long satisfaction of breathing in,
the only obligation of the moment;
the pause, a radiating
momentary absence of need.
There is nothing to excite
nothing to distract;
the unadorned disfunctional solids
that pervade the oily ether
discourage discovery.
Here, with relief,
all needs are muted,
their distinctions neutered,
where greater freedoms are made welcome,
with the responsibility of choice.
There are no preferences in this addiction,
the need to think is relieved of duty,
satisfactions triumph over hesitations,
and nothing awkward blunts this pleasure.

# THE CHOICE

It is not the actions of choice
but the earlier wallowing in expectation,
that outlines the moment,
the odd tingle, the movement,
the current from head to heart to loin;
the hand that makes a gesture
so swift to be nearly unseen,
perhaps unconscious,
that adjusts an unruly spot below a waist,
giving rise to a moment,
a thought, a projection of what's in wait.

Oh, how we will kiss,
and be kissed,
and how the ears,
not needing to strain,
will hear the intimate breath of ecstasy,
so near the warmth penetrating our ears
with the sound of sheets and afternoons.

And then there is the heart
that is the companion of the body,
the heart that operates the eyes,
that paints with spots and wrinkles,
forging love from heat
and submission.

## AGOG IN BANTER

The poets and those who banter,
are agog in phrases.
Through imperfect memory, and interest,
not always reciprocated,
transmissions sometimes abrupt, or incoherent,
our precision made hesitant by pain,
we listen for each other in nights
still and dense with fog and moonlight.
Our awareness steeped in longing,
unions too quickly sated by repetition
and presumption.
Intimacies fetishized, abbreviated,
circumscribed in orbits gone amok
from earlier mornings of sunlight
and disordered sheets.

## THE GAMBLE

I am reckless,
and wager all that I have,
against the inevitable end.
This, I do, in a rush of pleasure.
I relish the game,
at the table, alert,
not placid or resigned.
I am living.
I defy the fates, and the gods,
or anyone's only god;
and defy, as well, the clock.
Defeated, I will walk away calmly,
depleted, but for a moment, of resources,
with a mind that returns determined,
again, to win against the odds,
not suffering or lingering in loss.
Mindful that the game is where the energy resides,
where the drive to persist fires the engine.
Wakeful, I push to the center,
not with optimism but instinct.
My hopefulness is intact,
but aches, now, with overuse.

# THE SKIN OF OUR SEEKING

For long, I thought
that it was love
that ruled the world;
it had been so powerfully proposed,
so eagerly adopted
by righteous believers.

It was so fused to the skin of our seeking,
I had hoped for it to be true,
and pinned my timid certainty
to its promise,
only to be deflated,
again and again,
by love's failure to endure.
I fall back, in soft comfort,
onto the wedding beds of words,
reciting phrases and litanies,
strands released from double helixes,
the mutterings of ageless poets,
watching as eagerness dissolves
callous, and pleasure repurposes doubt.

# THE VILLAINY OF SUCCESS

In the knuckles of my recall
there is the pain, now, of all that I've
hit against and grasped.
I feel it at first light,
when all is still,
and the duties of the day begin their cascade.
The pain is carried into the tasks,
harbingers of decline.
Remnants of the strength needed
to be witnessed and handled.
It is a hot ache that arrives in cool rushes,
and attends, with all the other thoughts,
the obligation to distractions,
the relentless and terminal sacrament of duty.
Our minds, our personal interiors,
always yearn for something else,
something other than what's at hand,
something more or less than anything near.
The nature of distraction is to be relentless,
as its duty can never reach the satisfactions
of fulfillment, despite the villainy of
success.

# THE HAUNT OF DEPRESSION

Being completely resistant
to the compulsion of moving forward.
Being disinterested.
Not caring.
Being repulsed by inspiration,
and the consequent shirking of responsibility,
the attendant guilt,
fomented by the knowledge
that intention has been overtaken
and suppressed by the lassitudes of inaction,
by the unnatural darkening of rooms,
the muting of colors,
the repulsion of exuberance
the denial of enthusiasm,
to the recriminating justification that
joy is obviously and deliberately thwarted.
That the inclination toward tenderness is made
to be suspicious and menacing,
that trust has been subverted by
the certain knowledge of betrayal,
and worst of all that likeability and
self-esteem have never been real.
That the health of others is a threat,
that unsuppressed laughter is always a taunt,
that hypocrisy is the bottom-line motivator
for every phrase, every comment,
every attempt at community
and communication.

# RELICS

We are evidence,
relics in the reserves of existence.
As the waiting never begins,
never ends,
we turn ourselves back,
into reflected light,
light that beckons to a future,
when we no longer see the skies,
and we are found in remnants
amidst shiny objects and dust,
decipherable, perhaps,
by those with similar curiosities
and familiar questions,
seeking, in their own misbegotten void,
for occasional relief from uncertainty,
taking readings from our wounds,
enabling their own predictions.
What we now know as love and knowledge
will lie encoded in the future's sifted sand.

# DEFEAT

Steeped in unworthiness,
and ending with the shock
of unimaginable defeat and harm,
this has been a terrible year.
Awakening, we are forced to suffer
the humiliation of our denials.
We pretended that we lived
amidst friends, civilized neighbors,
cultured, sensitive to all our colors,
all the benefits of sharing our daily bread.
But we were not.
We live in a global miasma
of swarming others.
In our houses we live together
in tense contempt:
for our sexual differences,
for unregulated desire,
our age disparities,
for our varieties of beliefs and interest,
for the smells we send aloft from our food.
Our faces are dense with indifference,
the outer skin nearly dead, crusty,
hosting the parasites that migrate from our feet
up to what might have been our souls,
save for the clamor for our distinctions.
What is this imperfect waiting we bear for
the solid warmth of love, for the hot kisses
of acceptance, for long strokes of each other,
for the join?

## THE BRINK

There is a long afternoon now
in which I live almost constantly,
a peaceful time
ever on the brink
of a sudden fall into sleep.
It is a pillow,
soft and smelling sweetly
of breezes, rustling leaves,
and the shadows of clouds.
It sucks my attention into a dream,
a suddenness that dissolves
and disrupts itself,
jolts me alert
so that I am surprised in my chair.
I have a thought of my age
and the dooming edge
the cut-off, the drop.
In that, a strange comfort
urges me to draw a few lines
onto the page of this day.
I shift, look out,
mindful of the West,
the sinking light
and the grateful promise
of another day.

## WINE ON THE DECK

Over wine,
on the famous deck
with a view to the sea
I asked a languorous poet
to succinctly define humanity:
"So, humans are, each, unique
instruments of calibration
in an experiment
of self-consciousness,
made possible
by time and local elements,
with an unfathomable purpose,
in an indifferent expanse:
complex, expendable, unvenerated."
He smiled, it appeared,
happy at the thought.

# FINISH WHAT?

He never knew if he could finish.
Still doesn't.
Time was something to be aware of.
Like the smell of early coffee,
or settling into the seat of a plane.
He stood to the side of its affects.
Not that he didn't get older,
and weaker, and not that he didn't
make choices.
But, for him, it was infinite.
No decisions were urgent.
But he never knew if he could finish.
He was a place.
Not an item or a person.
His place was on the move.
He made the choice to know it.
And made a life of hours.
He was atoms in a streak.
Not seen. Not utilized for insight.
But made for making tracks.
Proof for nothing that cares to be known.
Replication.
What this does.
Not fate.
Hinting of certainty, sustained by immensity.
Clarities of justice.
One justice exceeding others,
moment to moment.
A justice without lack.
A stand for the moment.
Looking out with innocent eyes.

## SPAWN OF BARNUM

A small sadness lurks
in every joy,
the shadow part
in dappled sunlight;
some whisperings
of what words we'd mutter
if we knew they'd be welcome.
Fear is now the new possibility.
We shelter in pods of it,
we wipe it off like the sweat
from our faces,
onto the legs of our pants.
We arrange our days with it,
going out proudly
with the ingenuity of self-deception.
Endless possibilities of it,
like lists of actors' birthdays,
entertain our disheartened depths.
Fear, of everything,
now crowns our creativity,
strutting eager plans for achievement,
despite the noisy pressure of hopes
gone over to fakery.
Positive thinkers,
now the adopted step-children
of Barnum's suckers,
are shamed by legions of certainty's minions.

## HER CHILD

In those early days there was only one woman to love.
We had long afternoons
in the serene vicinity of her silent work.
I learned that life was the smell
of steam, rising from the press of
newly washed fabric,
and that even more, there was the board,
still warm to my face, first one side,
then the other, and that I loved to climb it.
I learned that life was all that lingered
in the air when her fingers were finished,
the machine and scissors put away,
and when the sun reached down
and all the suspended motes became stars,
her eyes attached to mine.
She spoke our secret language of assurance,
her mind flooded all my heart;
the ritual was that we must nap
against each other,
she my giant in afternoons
that reeked of infinity
and everything would float and mingle
in the soft, humid furnaces
of our endless invention.

## TO POSTPONE

Immortality is the experience
of being alive
while also certain
of the great fiction of death.
This is unteachable,
unmoved by the rigors of aspiration,
contemptuous of hope.
Not sharable, only known with solitude.
What the mind extrudes through the skin,
the rind of beingness,
is personal.
There are no loops in immortality.
The genius in every moment
is deciphered through the flaws.
Flaws are the background against which
the unsurpassed is noticed.
Awareness of perfection is fragile, short-lived,
like orgasm, not meant to endure:
sparks meant to instigate the healthy humors of desire.
Desire is the generator of will,
and we know our vitality in postponement.

## GAPS

In every mindful soul,
there are awkward gaps,
between the idealism in desires
(incessant)
and the reality of fulfillment
(periodic).
We dwell, mostly,
in the gaps.

# DEFAULT

The default currency of the horde is trivia.
The aggregate impulse of society,
any society,
is goodness.
The striations in the thick fabric of atavism,
pretentions to prominence,
the choices are, at first, to remain hidden,
to dart beneath the leaves,
to scuttle, to remain, merely, the sound of retreat,
to be gone before the judging eye has turned.

# SHUDDERING IN PLACE

Scattered around us
as if an unexpected wind
has just visited with malign fury
are the upended chairs and tables of yesterday's
feasting in the unsuspecting sun.
Cups and saucers, a whisky glass,
a sweater, whose?
Disorder now taunts us
and bids us to make new place settings in its midst.
We are abandoned by all the neat and tidy history,
the comfy tales of our noble heritage,
and the (always tentative) hope and conviction
that our work and planning would carry us aloft
to the soft perch from which we would
dim and fade and die
in sight of our loved ones faces.
Hands entwined in the near comfort of love.
Not to be.
Our own words have taken a march,
and new and sinister meanings have usurped the old:
justice, custom, dignity, truth, veneration, respect,
have all taken a powder,
and are on an aimless walk outside our shuddering bodies.

## A YEARNING TO WRINKLE

To break the spell of another *today*
I put on a special shirt;
crisply pressed,
proud of its perfection,
ready for the arena.
It made its way to my daily chair,
and innocent of guile began with purpose:
it purported to be once again at large,
in the world of men and women,
buying, planning, scheming, celebrating,
stealing little intimacies,
shrouding secret pleasures in common lies,
sharing random meals, running errands,
running this, running that, running!
But, really, no longer.
My shirt now takes longer to wrinkle,
and feels a longing to be stained over moments of wine,
hopes in vain for a nearby face to share
in the explosion of a laugh, and listens in despair
to overhear a conversation not meant for it.
It's desperate for an airing in a din,
and then a satisfying drive home, anticipating a change
into something more comfortable,
and a reason to be sent off for its routine cleansing
and renewal.  It yearns for the casual tossing,
to the floor, to the heap, and the drawstring sack;
the cycle, the routine, the weekly play of choices
and *replay*.

## BLANTONS OR KNOB CREEK

She leaned into the cushions,
turned to see if I was listening,
"There are a few men
I still have sex with,
it can be said that we've
cultivated each other.
Over time.
We are no longer enticing.
But that does not matter.
Old sex is rarely attractive.
We still enjoy some playful stalking,
like nocturnal creatures,
desperate to bloom,
one more time,
wondering,
when our heads fall off to the side,
will this be the final rush?
I was sustained,
in between chances,
which often felt somewhat long,
by knowing that there would come an end,
soon perhaps, as time went on,
of that hollow longing.
Yes, then, we behaved, as before,
like animals.
Beginnings were never graceful;
we would tear into each other.
But the aftermath,
had dignity.
We had known each other,
we had even given
what was usually withheld.
We let be active
what duty and shame demanded
we suppress, keep hidden.

It always came to mind,
when I was naked, open,
aghast at my passion,
that this ripe and sweaty intimacy
is more powerful
than any act of faith.
That our bodies,
no longer young displayed
the true and unpolluted might
of human effort and meaning.
Not to be worshipped or enshrined
by the dominating clever,
but for all the purposes
of simple caring, of loving,
to gain some footing in courage,
and to ritualize the ecstasy
of being alive."

Her glass was empty,
she shifted her knee
off the arm of her perch
and motioned to me with her head
for more.

## UNKNOWN OTHERS

A misshapen bewilderment
stands at the door
of every morning.
It is an agonizing blur.
It does not speak,
or gesture in any direction
that can be deciphered.
In the lingo of the moment
it signifies the universal *whatever*.
It carries no accent of time,
and our defiance of it
is saturated with impotence.
There is nothing to do:
the posture is all there is,
when no meaning can be seen
on a face.
A hesitant stumble
is now the animated emoji
of all those who have so easily,
defiantly, and stupidly, refused to
any longer be responsible
(as if they ever were).
And now we see them lose their hero
and we are tugged at our hearts.
Some learn, and some don't,
and we are angry, but everyone must be saved,
so we pull them up.
Already we know the false repentance
that oils our regret.  Come, dine with us.
We, too, are weary of toil and misunderstanding,
of surviving, second after second,
the shared terror
of the unknown selves,
and the always unknown others.

## GUESS AGAIN

It is your best guess
about God
against all the others.
Your position does not stop time,
nor signal a spot of reason.
Little orgasms of certainty,
fireflies of pleasure,
are markers in the plotting of time,
as we continue the study.
Of course, there will be
another moment,
just like this,
from another chair,
near another window,
the rain will pick itself up,
(no, not mindlessly)
and follow you,
 (innocently)
and not be surprised
at your choices.

## A DEATHBED

In the minutes before she died
I could see time writing on her hands:
runic signs all over them,
spots, and veins,
the damage of heartbreak,
wreckage from years of work,
skin gone translucent
by the march of seasons,
bones no longer delicate
but swollen from the incessant
rhetoric of arthritis.
And yet,
at rest,
one enfolded with the other
witness to a temporary serenity,
priming to throb again
in the dull pain
the attempt at a gesture,
they seemed sculpted by grace.
Her fingers,
no longer strong
are symbols of loss
nearing the finish line of duties;
the tears wiped,
the lips smoothed,
the hair fixed,
all the delicate tasks of
ensuring a look.

## OLD FRIENDS

We occupy our afternoon chairs.
And in our ritual sitting
we cradle memories of being young.
Pictures of us as youngsters
are flashing before our separate realities,
and we feel, for a moment,
that we still inhabit that once undaunted freshness,
that undeniable lonely glory,
when innocent of our beauty,
we had been surprised to be surprised;
we feel no erosion of skin or certainty,
and we flood each other
with the love of all beginnings,
the beginnings which still linger between us,
little sprouts of peculiarity and habit,
the space where all the unspoken phrases
a few ghosts of gestures not made,
kindnesses only intended, never achieved,
sustain the illusions of love,
family, friendship,
and solitude.
The silence settled at last
and seemed generous,
and the long stretch of waiting
turned and groaned
with deep satisfaction.
A communion of insight
settled within us.

## GENEROUS SIP

Can you feel this with me?
The bourbon sinking in,
nosing through my roots.
These are the early moments,
the hot brilliance of a generous sip;
here, now, the loosening of the
incessant grip of survival's constant diligence,
the release of that nameless something
a personal persistent architecture
so necessary, so constant, yes, yes, gone;
my eyes now see through closed lids
and my chair has become a close friend.
There is success in all that creation has
meant for us, especially the incarnation
of benevolent pulsing, so very sweetly,
from my center, where all the
landscapes are glorious,
where spring is always in full flush for poets:
all working artists are overflowing
with prosperity, are diligent with purpose,
and have not yet been overwritten
by despair, or congregant fear.
Someone should paint this.

## SHADES UP

So, as if in a fit,
I opened all the shades,
all the windows,
and let the pristine light
from the landscape
work its wonder on my soul.
In came the undulating hills,
the trees,
the oblivious cattle,
chewing, chewing,
strolling, shitting,
revitalizing where they walk,
settling their lack of urgency
on me.

## AN EDIT

Now I know that I will edit
to the end.
On my last breath surely I will need to insert a comma,
or at least grant an ellipsis.
I will require,
if you are still a reader,
that you make the effort to pause
(in deference to the next required action)
and wait,
for there will certainly be an insight
that comes of *your* own pausing,
that manifests from the movement,
well beyond our comprehension,
that gave rise to this movement
which will never be contained
and wants nothing in return.

## SWEET SHARDS OF DARK CHERRIES

Here we are
come a summer's day,
languid with knowledge,
following some drifting seeds.
A life of instinct and chance.
Origins soaked in the turmoil
of haphazard impulses.
Links in a chain of experimentation
with the occasional relief of alcohol.
Concentric flushes of skin on skin,
kissing that claimed the endurance of hours,
punctuated by a babble of shared breathing,
gasping in and out,
laughing too,
the taste of ice and bourbon
and the sweet shards of dark cherries.
We were the lucky ones,
we few,
who took the time
and never feared the waiting.
Sequestering trysts from hours of duties,
routines,
and the silliness in purposes
that once dotted
and marred
our schedules.

## SHELTERING

Now, in these primitive moments
the mystery is manifest
in a distilled isolate,
in the fires of what was once
obvious,
and is no longer hidden:
in the unshaven face,
or one with no make-up,
in the fatigue of another day,
a routine in service to doubt.
Do we who are now without fire
make offerings? A sacrifice to our
lives gone before?
How then do the daily gods serve
in a stricken world,
our lands so dense with
all that has been forgotten?
But not forgotten:
how lovely is our spirit,
and the faces of our children.
Not forgotten:
the gift of all our celebrations,
and wonder.
The days are at play as if we've no
reason to reply to each other.
We just are.
The trick being played
is one in which the removal of doubt
is made to seem real,
and our bedrock, doubt,
now under assault,
shelters only a biding time.
We are living the experiment,
without an engineer,
in the chronic abuse of delirium.
What's left is merely a phrase;

not one to be seized,
but one to rest upon,
to roll languidly upon our unified tongues.
We are packed in a world
cut off from any customary
shared agreeability,
and plunked back upon ourselves.

## CHANGING STACKS

Thousands and thousands of books have
moved wavelike through changing stacks
in all the rooms of my life:
years at play in a flickering moviola
freely called an education.
Powering advances through time
and circumstances,
doing the good and necessary work
of providing an illusion of success,
accomplishment, perspective, insight,
and only now as age eclipses routine
do I question or doubt the strength,
the reliability, of these edifices of conclusion;
the dancefloors on which, giddy in a personal music
of certainty, I throbbed and sweated with the best,
in an ecstasy, possible in only that moment,
an eyes-closed spectacle of visceral pleasure,
fragile witness to a youthfulness
spending itself
without regard to any future fears,
mindless of the threat of forgetting,
hapless of planning,
but confident, always,
that images would be endless,
both provocative and instructive,
never failing as fuel for living
and for the pulsing vitality of being alive.
Accepted was the mostly secret invitation
to humanity, and I placed myself,
perhaps too tepidly,
but at least visibly,
in the dance.
I was a solid block of dense and timorous
potential, and I carved a self out of that
from within.
Random, haphazard, mostly arcane

instructions came from those books.
But the touch of hands,
the coaxing and persistence
took hold of me,
aroused me
(not like the books)
with deliberate effort.
They waited when I held back,
when I ran,
and eased me back to freedom.

# FORTS

Born to the serenity of rural life
sequestered from noise
let loose upon entire days
in humid summer air
amused at every turn
surveying neighbors from endless sidewalks
visiting houses smelling of alien food
friends
and by turns instant enemies
forts
treehouses
and backyard secrets

## A TAUNT OF CLUES

Hidden in full view
is the universal taunt of the obvious:
that which will go on,
that which will endure,
the that of injustice,
the smug entitlements
that won't be entirely dislodged:
the fixed wealth
sustained by its size
and protections permitted in secrets.
But slowly
like lumbering cows on sultry days
we collude from underneath
in the erosion of those elite fetters.
For what is hidden wants to be seen,
and those who demand to know
will forever burrow
into all the dense and spiteful shrouds
that in their futility
purport to hide what will be known.
Instinct is a giddy and delicious guide.

## A GENTLE DEATH

So when she died,
just before,
the old woman looked up
and saw my look
and she always knew
that in my face
was always a question.

Her eyes closed
and she gently spoke,
"…to have been loved
was all that I knew,
and it is enough…
for all the rest."

I knew her eyes,
and finally, we met with our eyes,
and, suddenly, I could not see.

Some fabric, now, stands in for her,
shards and remnants sewn in a patchwork,
embraceable, wafting faintly of her hands,
and her gentle craft,
some molecules dispersing,
giving up what once was the integrity
of a life,
the vital gift of grace
in the actions of nurturing
and unbroken attention.

## AN OBVIOUS RESET

In what sliver of sky and air
do we stand, arms at our sides,
(the western namaste)
signaling respect for our *others*?
Where is space in lives
all who matter?
How do we overcome
the daily recurrence of naivete
that builds like the crust in our eyes
during regular nights of fitful sleep?
There is now a sudden recognition
of the obvious:
that every moment contains the *all*
of our tiny lives.
All our previous attempts at sorting,
and analyzing,
all by the purity of their essences,
has yielded only the daily reset to zero,
which is, really, the most gigantic advantage
we wake up to
and instantly ignore.

## ARDOR IN PLACE

I wonder now, how much longer the kissing will last.
Every moment is an anniversary of some love gone.
To age is to carry all the weight of memory,
again, each day, piles of fading pleasures,
on shoulders failing in strength,
frail now, with hesitation and longing.
But do not turn away from these gifts from time.

Lean into the kisses as do the young,
though our glance to the side might
be ripe with shyness.
Our beauty, now not imposing,
bereft of the firmness that once furnished
our faces with the colors of desire,
are creased by experience, loss,
and dread.

But, open, anyway, toward the gladness
of being seen, and the sudden knowledge
that waiting has always been the enduring
comfort and joy within all the chances
that love offers in each and all the kisses.

Where once was the gasp, is now the whisper,
and the kiss, perhaps the last, is still the wonder.
Relish the sudden warmth that
awakens your tongue; surrender to its probing,
remember, in an instant, again, the impenetrable
nearness of each moment, and its instant vanishing,
as every pleasure yields to its demise,
and renders hot gratitude
to the cool toiling of memory.

## SUMMER FLIES

Suddenly, dragonflies!
And with them lightning in the night,
their attention caught like
floating seeds might occasionally
be snagged by the outer edges of all things larger.
Then in hours of random action
get pounded down,
coaxed by wind or rain
into the granular womb of earth
where the miracle of all seized circumstances
allows life to converge
with the chance for survival
in warmth
and humid folds of darkness.
And now those of us awake
in this constant
middle-of-time
are amazed that it does
and that it doesn't sprout forth,
distinct, identifiable,
doomed to brevity.
But, wait, do some of us still hold books
in welcoming laps?
Does not every afternoon offer up reliable
hours of calm?
For a few months I carried Lydia Davis
around on my back.
She was a **great** weight.
I trust her to know
how these words should be translated,
for meanings to be accurately realized.
She endorses my freedom
to trust in readers.
She joins a chorus of influencers,
advisors, inspirers
whose work has worked

in the living guise of print
to sanction moments in my day
of searing pleasures
of phrases, strung by fools on the loose,
launderers of socks and shrouds,
poets stringing lines in the wind,
flapping loony shapes,
comic bait with good purpose,
that hope and imagination, together,
do not stop playing, playing, playing.

# FOR NOW

Outside, a crow is making a meal of a fledgling bird. Its purpose is dutiful and heartless and is carried out with the same severe alacrity displayed by its slick black plumage. It fled with some of its meal in its mouth, dropping untidy fluffy tufts and blood, when I surprised it by approaching. Every moment of time like this one contains within it the approach, and the surprise to its gist.

One mystery of life, at least seemingly, is that it is incorrigibly disordered. And what we do, all that we do, is a speaking back to the forces and patterns that have conspired to foment our emergence. The miracle is that we pull totalities out of our moments, out of random phrases in our minds. And that's what poetry is for me: pulling totalities out of random phrases. But, for this, ironically and disastrously, we writers must relinquish any notion of control and leave that miracle as the remit of readers. A word once lifted from a yearning heart, or wrenched in anguish from a mind in turmoil, becomes a floating orphan of possibility, a mote at dance in all the shafts of light, in all the days, that all we are granted to awaken and play in.

The phrases are fleeting, and if you are not in the moment with them, then like the burst from a firefly, they are gone, wiped from memory. For some poets, the glimpse of a phrase is the only reliable evidence of reality. The phrases arise from within the singularity of an individual, are unique to that instant, that person, and maintain their burst, their light, only upon recognition, which for some (if not all) only comes later. A time removed from an instant. If we suffer our memories, it is because they are in tardiness to reality, which is ever slipping through (some say away from) us as instantaneously as it seems, moment by moment, to be happening. It is a wonder that in this constantly extending miasma of neither here nor now we are able to adjust, with any coherency, and *recognize* our lives.

Here is birdsong: a gentle hand that caresses our face; the warmth of an embrace that reaches through to our surprised soul, awakened in thanksgiving that love can still reach us, so far have we drifted from its gifting, so oblivious have we become to its permanence. And (here is where we struggle like worms on a hook) we must work against the terrible impermanence of each and every pleasure of body and mind that might have come our way. Poetry is the surest, finest, way to not be alone. Both writing it and reading it. Poetry is any speaking aloud that annihilates oblivion. So, speak to live, and listen, to be recognized.

## THE DRIFT


What strength is left for us?
This silent, glorious house,
perhaps about to burn, signals no anguish,
or remorse, or terror.
It waits for searing heat
to give up its atoms
in horrific billowing smoke,
and with fierce wind,
take an almost joyful ride
toward random distant fields,
to settle again,
and wait
then rise up to the sun
as something else.

I can actually hear
the falling ash.
It's soft, has no shame or regret,
lands sure of itself,
the gist of its purpose resolved,
accomplished,
being now the visible aftermath
of homes, lives, trees, memories,
routines,
the snow from their simpler illusions,
floating, drifting, ghostly moments,
never to appear again as before.
Muses for millions of new acres of memory,
oracles of warning,
declaring in the grace of drifting
that whatever is spared has no place
to rest easy.

*Charlie Pendergast, 2018*

**Charlie Pendergast** was born in Superior, Wisconsin. He began a career in writing at the age of nineteen, after moving to Los Angeles. He previously wrote feature articles for in-flight magazines and was associate editor of *Motor Trend Magazine,* among other jobs. His first book *Introduction to Organic Gardening* (Nash, 1971) was published in several editions.

Pendergast's previous poetry books are *A Commonplace of Poetry* (RiskPress, 2010) and *Gone Untreated* (RiskPress, 2018). He and his partner Kevin Connor administer the RiskPress Foundation, which has as its mission to seek out, support, and produce the work of emerging artists, particularly poets and other writers. He lives happily in rural Northern California surrounded by redwoods and the sound of ecstatic cows.

# THE PAGE POETS SERIES

Number 1
*Between First & Second Sleep* by Tamsin Spencer Smith

Number 2
*The Michaux Notebook* by Micah Ballard

Number 3
*Sketch of the Artist* by Patrick James Dunagan

Number 4
*Different Darknesses* by Jason Morris

Number 5
*Suspension of Mirrors* by Mary Julia Klimenko

Number 6
*The Rise & Fall of Johnny Volume* by Garrett Caples

Number 7
*Used with Permission* by Charlie Pendergast

# Dedication

To my mother, who taught me that love is an action verb and not a noun. She modeled how I should show love by giving flowers to people while they are living, sending someone a card to celebrate all holidays (and always making sure money is in the card), spending time with family and friends, and telling someone you love them as much as possible. Thank you, Mama, for all the sacrifices you made to make sure our family had its needs as well as its wants met. You always did everything out of love. I lost my mother on December 29, 2019, but God gained an angel. I miss my mother with all my heart, but I know she watches over me every day. I thank you for being YOU, and for modeling what love looks like in action. I love you, Mama!

To my daughter: I loved you from the moment you entered this world on February 18, 1990. As a seventeen-year-old, I didn't have a plan as to how to raise you, but God already had it all mapped out. My daily prayer has always been to show you how much I love you and to model how to love others unconditionally. I knew I would never be a perfect mother, but I would try my best to be half the mother my mother was to me. I think you are the most beautiful person in the world, both inside and out. I now pray you will be the best mother to your children. I love you, Tyra.

# The Writing Style:

I have been saying I would love to write a book about quotes that could empower people. For four years, I would start and stop for a variety of reasons. I even had the majority of the book written in 2017, but my laptop crashed, and I lost everything. I saw this as God's way of telling me to start over; this is not the direction for you at this time.

As it turned out, another direction for my book came about in 2018! I decided to choose my favorite personal quotes while highlighting people in my life that epitomize and model each quote. I strongly believe that you should tell someone how they have impacted your life while you are living, so this is the "why" behind the structure of my book. I challenge each person who reads this book to think about a person who epitomizes and models each quote and TELL them, or simply think about how you model this quote.

Another thought came to mind as I finally wrote my book: What legacy do I want to leave behind? Fear of the unknown encouraged me to stop talking about it and make it happen. As my beloved mother, Doris Jenkins Flood, was called to her heavenly home on December 29, 2019, I was then again reminded that her legacy was love and that I, too, want to be remembered for the love I have shown to others.

I hope this book is confirmation of the love I have for each of you, and if I didn't highlight your words in this publication, don't worry; my future is bright. Until the next book, remember: Your words have also encouraged me. I love you and I pray that I've shown you just how much.

I encourage you to read the book with a purpose. As you read, question how you model love and how you show love to others.

After reading this book of daily quotes, if one resonates with you, please send me an email to share, as I would love to hear from you: CFlood700@gmail.com.

# 30 Life Changing Quotes: Personal Narratives

*"Home is where my story begins" by Shirley Cook.*
*Hometown: Rich Square, North Carolina*

**Dr. Christa L. Flood**

# 1

*"For every problem, there is a solution"*

**~ Author Unknown.**

(This quote applies to Tyra Janay Flood, my one and only daughter.)

Becoming a single mom at the age of 17 changed my life forever—for the best. Initially, I thought only about how immature, young, and financially unstable I was and how this would negatively impact my daughter's life. However, with supporting parents, siblings, and friends, Tyra grew to be a successful young woman who will be bringing my first grandson into the world this year!

I have witnessed my daughter look at all problems as opportunities to find a solution. I often say, "Tyra can do it." I say this because I watched Tyra leave college to pursue her dream of becoming an entrepreneur, but after she realized it wasn't the best decision, she returned to college and completed her undergraduate degree at Winston-Salem State University. Then, I watched her decide to relocate to New York, just because she had always wanted to live there. As her mother, I was so scared and nervous about her moving to the "Big Apple," but once again, Tyra found a way to make a living and stayed there for three years. Then, I watched her decide to relocate to

Houston, Texas to work with animals. In my heart, I was nervous once again, but she would always say, "I got this." She did have it! She followed her dream of working with animals and relocated to Texas, which has now been her home, and her husband's home, for four years.

Am I a proud mother? Beyond proud, because I feel confident that for every problem that comes her way, Tyra will find a solution.

Are you looking for solutions or only thinking about the problems?

# 2

*"Are you an asset or a liability?"*

## ~ Author Unknown

(This quote applies to Towanda S. Macon, line sister of Delta Sigma Theta Sorority and long-time friend.)

"Tee," as we often call her, came into my life in 1992, when we entered Winston-Salem State University as excited and eager freshmen. We were both heavily involved in campus activities and lived in the same dorm on the same floor, so our interactions became frequent. In 1994, our connection grew even closer when we both pledged with Delta Sigma Theta Sorority, Inc.

I recall we studied together, attended events together, and took time to learn about one another. Many of our stories, we quickly realized, were often one and the same! We felt like no one else understood rural America and the places that reared us. We identified with limited resources and having "good old country" parents who gave all of what they had to ensure that we were a little bit better. Tee always gave back in some way, whether by volunteering in the Forsyth County community, helping others on campus, or creating clever ways to fill our hungry stomachs.

Tee has always made family and community her top priorities. It is no surprise that today she works assisting people in impoverished areas throughout the state of Illinois, and she is an advocate for ensuring people have decent housing and essential resources. In 1995, my father passed away, and Tee, along with my line sisters, drove five hours to support me during my bereavement. She has always been an asset to everyone she knows. A few years ago during one of our long catch-up chats, we were sharing about God's blessings on our lives, and she modestly confided that she was planning to purchase a home for her parents. Today, her parents reside in the home she purchased.

When I think of Towanda S. Macon, I instinctively ask myself, "Are you an asset or a liability?" She not only talks the talk, but she has always walked the walk by being an asset toward family, friends, and her community.

Are you an asset or a liability?

# 3

*"Teamwork really makes the dreamwork"*

**~ John C Maxwell.**

(This quote applies to Kimberli Darling, Teach For America alumnae, mentee, and one of the six finalists for Teacher of the Year for Charlotte Mecklenburg Schools [CMS], 2020.)

I met Kimberli in 2012 when she started her teaching career as a Teach For America corps member, the same year I started working at Teach For America. To know Kimberli is to know a person who loves, supports, and challenges her students to reach their full potential. Kimberli is the wife of a teacher and the mother of four little darlings. She has modeled how to galvanize parents, students, colleagues, and the community through her soft but loud voice and with high expectations. You will find her leveraging various stakeholders' gifts and talents and collaborating to ensure goals are being met.

Her willingness to listen attentively to the perspectives of others and incorporate decisions being made, from lesson-planning to leading numerous initiatives at her school, speaks volumes about her approach to teamwork. She volunteers to lead professional development sessions with teachers to model best practices that she has learned throughout her teaching career. She leads with a growth- and an asset-based mindset. Kimberli's student achievement in math data is some of the highest in the school district.

To top off her career, she was selected as "Teacher of the Year" for two consecutive years at Cochrane Collegiate Academy, in 2016 as a middle school math teacher, and then again in 2020 as a high school math teacher. In 2020, she was selected as the "Teacher of the Year" for the Central I Learning Community and was one of six finalists in a school district that employees over 10,000 teachers. This places her at the 99th percentile among teachers within CMS!

She never wants to take credit for any accomplishments, even winning the prestigious award for her school and learning community, and will humbly tell you it was a team effort. Throughout numerous conversations with Kimberli, I have been impressed with her humility, perseverance, grit, and commitment towards students, and if you have the opportunity to meet her, you will surely experience the same thing.

How many of you lead from a teamwork approach?

# 4

*"You can feed the problem or a solution; whichever you feed is the one that will grow"*

**~ Toni Gaskins.**

(This quote applies to Kevin Poirier, Teach For America alum, advocate for children, Multi-Classroom Leader-West Charlotte High School.)

If you ever have the esteemed pleasure to meet Kevin, you would know why he lives a life that epitomizes this quote. I met Kevin in 2012, my first year on the Teach For America staff, and he was a first-year teacher. I remember engaging in a lengthy conversation with him in the parking lot on the campus at Johnson C. Smith University, when he inquired about computer-based learning for students he would be teaching at the L.I.F.T. Academy. He wanted to connect with someone who had been doing the work, so he could prepare himself for the classroom. I remember thinking to myself, "This young man is going to do a good job with our students!" Little did I know that over the next eight years, he would surpass my expectations and not only do an amazing job for students but for our entire Charlotte community.

I feel as though I have worked alongside him, learned from him, and developed a great relationship over these years. Kevin has seen numerous problems, but he has intentionally decided to feed the solution, not the problems. He has consistently and strategically fought for equity for black and brown students and the communities they live in. A couple of years ago, one of my mentees didn't have a laptop to complete his assignments at home. He was working a part-time job and finishing his senior year, so I reached out to Kevin to inquire about how to solve this issue. Kevin immediately told my mentee to meet him, and he provided the laptop. My mentee went on to graduate from high school and to become the first in his family to attend college. This is only one story that serves as an example of how Kevin solves problems when there often seems like no other solution. May I add that Kevin doesn't allow his Caucasian ethnicity to dictate who he will and will not help.

Kevin serves as an advocate, servant leader, and humble man who will go to great measures to make sure educational injustice is dismantled on all fronts. You may see him participating at school board meetings, serving on panels that address systematic racism, and delivering technology/resources to students who lack them. One of his latest accomplishments is that he joined the mighty fraternity of Alpha Phi Alpha, with which his beliefs and core values align.

Will you feed the problem or solution? Kevin has decided that he will feed the solutions and not the problems that he encounters daily.

# 5

*"A delay is not a denial…"*

## ~ Author Unknown.

(This quote applies to Roberta Ingram, my long-time friend.)

My friend for years, Roberta, has used this quote since we first learned about it in many aspects of her life. She always says, "Roberta loves the kids." She has owned her own daycare facility for over twenty years, which she plans to do for another twenty years. However, one of her personal goals came to fruition when she yelled from the rooftop one day to ask me, "Can you attend my graduation?"

For years, Roberta had been on a start-and-stop cycle toward degree completion, seeking her degree for family reasons, and now her dream had become a reality when she graduated. I was reminded that if you don't accomplish something right away, it may just be a delay—it doesn't mean a denial. Life has a way of throwing us curve balls sometimes, but what you do with those curveballs is what matters. Remember to keep your eyes on the prize, and it may come to fruition, if a little later than expected. Congratulations, my friend, on a job well done.

Have you been denied something recently? Maybe it was just a delay.

# 6

*"Every setback is just a setup for a mighty comeback"*

**~ T.D. Jakes.**

(This quote applies to Carlos Diaz-Ramirez, mentee.)

Dr. Sheila Ijames is the former principal at the Harding Ram Academy, a school that allows students to use a computer-based program to catch up on work that they missed throughout the years in order to graduate. Dr. Ijames was recruiting volunteers to help seniors write their senior exit papers, so I decided to volunteer weekly.

Carlos was one of my former mentees who I had spent a year tutoring, mentoring, and getting to know. I recall my first meeting with Carlos; he was so energetic and positive about finishing all of his assignments and graduating from high school on-time. I asked him, "How did you get behind in your classes, and why did you decide to enroll at the Harding Ram Academy?"

Carlos shared how he had been hanging with the wrong crowd and making poor choices about school but desperately wanted a better life for himself and his family. Then he opened up to tell me that his mother had been deported back to his home country about two years prior, which shook his entire family. He shared that he and his little brother were being raised by his single father. These were the setbacks in his life. He vowed to set himself up for success, but he needed a little help. He told me his goal in life was to be the first high school graduate and college graduate in his family, which he identifies as being Hispanic. As I type this reflection, the hairs on my arm stand up because I can remember the passion in his voice as he talked.

We spent countless hours on his senior exit project, talked on the phone, and worked on his computer-based classes. I remember being excited to see Carlos every week, not only to work on his paper but because I knew he would also share stories about his family and his part-time job. Carlos ended up earning the second-highest score on his senior presentation; to say that he was excited would be an understatement. He felt so accomplished.

As the year ended, Carlos walked across the stage as the first high school graduate in his family and was accepted into Central Piedmont Community College for the fall. He had defied all odds by graduating from high school and entering college. He gleamed with joy when he walked across that stage with his family cheering him on. He said, "I told you I would do it, and thank you, Ms. Flood, for believing in me." I told him that, first of all, he believed in himself—that is what made the difference.

Students like Carlos exist all across the country. Who will you help to make their goals come true? A little time goes a long way when you make it a priority. Carlos thought I helped him, but he helped me to understand and value the importance of helping others. Three years later, I still spend time with Carlos and his family, and we remain in touch with one another.

# 7

*"I don't live to work; I work to live"*

**~ Noel Gallagher.**

(This quote applies to Claude "Quick" Morrison, a dear friend.)

To be honest, I constantly kept asking myself: Does Claude epitomize this quote? Finally, I was able to find the words to explain how he does. Claude came into my life in 2017, when the organization I was working for was using his school for a week-long professional development training over the summer. I was responsible for organizing a resource room where new teachers could sort through free supplies to start their classrooms. Therefore, I had to transport tons of supplies, such as storage bins, chart paper, lamps, chairs, carts, books, and many other resources to the school.

For weeks, Claude and I met in the front of the school to exchange supplies. Sometimes I would arrive at 5 am to start organizing the resources, and one day he asked, "Can I just drive my truck and meet you at your office to bring the resources back?" I told him it was my responsibility and that I wouldn't want him to take time away from his school. He insisted, but I stood my ground because I knew he was a busy man.

He shared conversations about his work hours. He arrived at work each morning by 4 am to get the building prepared for the students and staff, and he loved his job. He didn't see it as work; he saw it as a calling and a way to help as many people as possible, even when others found excuses to be absent from their work. He has shown me that when you find a job that you are passionate about, then you won't see it as work.

You can find Claude mentoring students, volunteering in the community, helping others in any way needed, donating to help organizations, and smiling along the way. He served in the military, worked with another company, from which he retired, and is now back to work at a school, setting himself up to retire in a comfortable manner. He balances by working to live, which gives him joy and peace. He will retire one day with peace of mind and a sense of knowing he has made a difference in people's lives.

Are you working to live or living to work?

# 8

*"If you don't build your dreams, someone will hire you to help build theirs"*

**~ Toni Gaskins.**

(This quote applies to Erica Jordan-Thomas, doctoral candidate, long-time friend, and former principal at Charlotte-Mecklenburg Schools, owner and founder of EJT Consulting LLC.)

Leader! Innovator! Trailblazer! EJT embodies these words and more. Since meeting her some ten years ago, I have seen her tenacity, passion, and drive to fight for equality for kids. She never shied away from engaging in difficult and uncomfortable conversations about race, privilege, and the inequality that has permeated our schools and our community. She served as a principal of a Title I middle school for three years, where she raised the academic outcomes for children, increased parental support, and brought community leaders into her school.

She didn't stop at building dreams for her students and staff; she went on to start her own business as an educational consultant. She started her consulting business in October 2017 by believing in her skills, knowing her worth as an African-American woman, and learning from others. I am so appreciative that she didn't allow excuses to keep her from building her dreams. She is a role model to so many, and the best is yet to come.

Have you decided to build your own dreams instead of continuing to build someone else's?

# 9

*"As I look back on my life, I realize that every time I thought I was being rejected from something good, I was actually being redirected to something better"*

**~ Steve Maraboli.**

(This quote applies to Starlet Deloatch, my niece.)

My niece, Starlet, and I are only nine months apart, which played a major role in our growing up like sisters instead of having the traditional aunt/niece relationship. We were always in school together, which also contributed to our closeness.

Starlet is the most intelligent woman I know in all arenas of life. She will tell you that any losses she experienced became lessons that she has taught her two beautiful daughters, Quiana and Natajah, as well as many other family members. She may have thought that at times, she was being rejected from something, but she was only being redirected to something better! She is a role model to me, as she has navigated through many tough times to come out victorious! I hope that she will continue to serve as a light in dark spaces for all who know and love her. She is my "light" in any dark space.

*Have you ever thought you were being rejected from something good but realized you were being directed to something better?*

# *10*

*"When it is your time to grow both personally and professionally, things will become uncomfortable"*

**~ Dr. Christa Flood.**

(This quote applies to Tomiaka Wingard, long-time friend and former colleague at Teach For America.)

I always tell Tomiaka I think she has a "secret crystal ball." In the four years I have known her, she has predicted events sometimes months before they have happened. When we were colleagues, I witnessed Tomiaka speak her truth and the truth of how black and brown children's voices are left out of the conversation. She would always ask, "Have we asked the children and their parents what they think?" This simple yet powerful question caused us to stop, reflect, and shift our actions in the moment. Everyone needs a Tomiaka in their workspace and life. Her questions will cause you to think twice and keep you focused on the real solution to the issue.

Two years ago, Tomiaka made a tough decision, which was to leave the staff and venture into a new position. It was difficult because she saw herself retiring from this organization, but she shared that in order to grow professionally and personally, the only way to truly embrace this hard decision was to step out on faith. In our numerous conversations, before and after she left the staff, she openly acknowledged that the feeling of being so uncomfortable helped her fulfill her mission and purpose in life. She was feeling scared, nervous, and doubtful while simultaneously experiencing feelings of freedom, peace, and hopefulness.

Now, I am here to share with you that she is striving and thriving in her new role, and she serves as a role model for others who share these same feelings. She typifies this quote in a genuine manner.

Will you run to or away from your dreams when you become uncomfortable? Are you continuing to stay in a place, whether professionally or personally, because you are afraid of being uncomfortable?

# 11

*"Don't mix up a seasonal relationship between a lifetime relationship"*

**~ Christa Flood.**

(This quote applies to Sandra Allgood, long-time friend.)

When I think about Allgood, yes, she is "ALLGOOD" and a friend for life. I met her years ago. We worked together in the Curriculum and Instruction Department. Not only did she possess a wealth of knowledge, but her calm spirit made her approachable. Have you ever met that person who just brings calmness and rationale to any situation?

I was the new staff member on the block, and Mrs. Allgood provided me with guidance and wisdom. Her guidance, understanding, and experience with supporting schools prevailed in her daily interactions and served as a model for me. Our friendship went deeper than a working relationship. It has been ten years of unconditional love and admiration. You may ask, how was this possible? It was possible because we intentionally continued to have phone conversations, scheduled monthly lunch dates, and social media interactions. If you want lasting friendships, you must be intentional and continue to water the seed that has been planted, and that was our commitment.

Who is someone you have remained friends with after your life or work shifted? How were you intentional about ensuring your friendship lasted? Key word: intentional.

# 12

*"You have three choices in life: Give up, give in, OR give it all you've GOT!"*

**~ Author Unknown.**

(This quote applies to Johnnie Williams, my brother-in-law.)

My brother-in-law is like an older brother to me. Our conversation topics vary. We talk about religion, politics, community activism, family values, and even the fluctuation of gas prices. He has an opinion about every topic and so do I, so we may run out of time but never run out of things to say.

In some families, "in-laws" may not have the best reputation, but I am here to officially dispel the myth and tell you that I have the best three brothers-in-law, and one is Johnnie. His nickname is "Frog," which I still need to find out the official origin of. I have always felt that because he jumps from pad to pad helping others, that's where his name came from. I guess that was all in my head.

Frog married my oldest sister, Zelma Williams, and he has been a blessing to my entire family. Just like a son, he helped both of my now-deceased parents in many ways, he has served as the mechanic in the family, and he financially supported his grandchildren as they matriculated and graduated from college. He wasn't raised in a wealthy family, but his hard work and love for God have allowed him to be an asset to hundreds of people, including family, friends, and the community. You can find him cutting grass at his church, picking up trash in his neighborhood, and helping someone move, all without any financial support. His attitude has remained consistent—that his rewards will come from heaven, not man.

Throughout his journey, he lost one of his best friends in a serious car accident, but he vowed to use this unfortunate death as motivation to give life everything he had and not to give up. Sometimes, losing a loved one can cause people to give up and see the world through a negative lens, but my brother-in-law used this as his way to be a leader in his community and a role model to others. His passion and drive to never quit have been an inspiration to me, as I have learned from him throughout my life. I just hope that my life, too, will be an example of not giving up and giving it all I have, no matter what the cost.

Will you make the intentional choice today to never give up, even when times get tough?

# *13*

*"The only place where success comes before work is in the dictionary"*

**~ Vince Lombardi.**

(This quote applies to Kendra Alston, long-time friend, author, sorority sister, and CEO of Koppertree, LLC.)

I asked Kendra, "Can I stay with you for a month until I am able to find my own apartment and relocate with my daughter to Charlotte?" Without hesitation, she said, "You sure can." Kendra, my line sister from Delta Sigma Theta Sorority, graciously allowed me to stay with her as I transitioned to Charlotte to start my professional career after college. I am forever indebted and grateful to her.

Kendra has always been kind-hearted, helpful, caring, visionary, and hardworking. She has been in education for over twenty years, and she continues to firmly believe that learning never stops. Her love and passion for kids have been consistent for years as I watched her lead step teams to win numerous competitions, mentor young girls and teachers, and move the academic dial for numerous children. I have seen her spend her money to purchase necessities for students without even thinking twice about it. Her hard work even resulted in writing her first children's book, entitled *Karson Goes to Kindergarten*. This amazing and uplifting book has been shared with students across the country. The icing on the cake was when Kendra stepped out on faith and started her own educational consulting company. It was hard work and dedication that led to her starting her own company. She is now a Black female entrepreneur who epitomizes "The only place where success comes before work is in the dictionary."

What are you currently working on that will ultimately yield success?

# 14

*"When you stop existing and you start truly living, each moment of the day comes alive with wonder and synchronicity"*

**~ Steve Maraboli.**

(This quote applies to Keon Artis, one of my nephews.)

To know my nephew is to know he models truly living, not simply existing. Keon is the oldest son of my brother, Deon, whom I love dearly also. All of Keon's life, he has set personal and professional goals and has accomplished them, one by one. Now, as an adult, he has been committed to working hard in his profession while traveling around the globe and has truly epitomized living a fun-filled life.

Keon has made it his life-long goal to plan trips that allow him to discover new cultures, experience local traditions, and connect with people around the world. While living out these goals, he posts on social media to bring these places into the lives of others, while encouraging others to live their best lives. One memorable trip was when he attended the 61st Annual Grammys! Seeing my nephew in the audience among some of the most famous people in the world reminded me that you can do whatever you want in life if you just go for it and just believe in yourself.

Family and friends often thank Keon for allowing them to see the world through his experiences, myself included, as we hope and dream to do the same. He volunteers at numerous events in the community as his way to pay it forward. He has set an example of how to be a young leader in the community and how to do it with a smile. You don't know where Keon may end up next on his journey, but I can promise you, he will show you how to "truly live and not simply exist" while on this earth.

Ask yourself, are you existing or truly living?

# *15*

*"Vision without execution is just hallucination"*

**~ Henry Ford.**

(This quote applies to Dr. Ronald Spencer Dixon, my mentor.)

"Spencer" is my mentor's middle name, and this is how I address him. As I reflected on this quote, Spencer was the first person who came to mind. He took a chance by hiring me in my first leadership role out of the classroom. At the time, he was the Assistant Superintendent for Middle School Curriculum and Instruction, and he hired me to serve as a Title I English/Language Arts coach. To say that I was taking a chance with this new role would be an understatement; I surely had the heart to lead adults but felt that I lacked the necessary skills.

For two years, Spencer taught me how to lead with both my head and heart. I knew he trusted and believed in me when several years later, he hired me in what would be my first assistant principal role in a Title I school in Charlotte, NC. I watched how his vision for children living in poverty came to fruition for two years under his leadership. He challenged and questioned systems that were not set up to allow children living in poverty to be successful. He let it be known that he believed in black and brown children and their families. I am indebted to him for showing me how to fight for educational equity for all children, no matter what the cost. He has helped numerous children and families by offering leadership and educational opportunities throughout his thirty years in education. Spencer is a true leader who models how a vision must be executed. If not, it will only be a hallucination—a mere thought.

What is your personal vision, and how have you executed it?

# 16

*"The only thing worse than being blind is having sight but no vision"*

**~ Helen Keller.**

(This quote applies to Shakeria Barnes, my long-time friend and former colleague at Bishop Spaugh Middle School.)

"Barnes" (as I used to address Shakeria) and I met at Bishop Spaugh Middle School years ago. It was the year 2010, and I was serving as an assistant principal. From the moment I met her, it was evident that Barnes was the kind of teacher who believed in children. She was teaching seventh grade English Language Arts, which just so happened to be my favorite subject. Her vision for helping scholars be on track to master reading skills was evident by her detailed lesson plans, as well as the way she executed them in her classroom. She had a resilient mentality, and her students knew they were expected to show up every day and excel in her classroom. We had numerous conversations about how she would use data to inform instructional delivery, leverage her parents, and develop as a teacher-leader.

Her drive and passion resonated on a daily basis. I witnessed Barnes spend her money to provide supplies and resources to students, plan activities, attend sporting events to support students, serve as PLC leader, and mentor young men and women, all while balancing being a mother of a young daughter and a supportive wife. It was never about Barnes. It was always about the children that she served. She made it known that the socioeconomic status of our students did not dictate expectations. Her vision as an educator was to ensure her students had equitable access to a quality education, regardless of their race and socioeconomic status.

We were only together for one year because the school board voted to close Spaugh Middle School along with nine other Title I schools on the west side of Charlotte. This was done in an effort to save money and support families more intensely by creating K-8 schools and developing a curriculum that was more aligned with those grade bands. When the news was released, Barnes was one of the teachers who rallied to help families, colleagues, and, most importantly, our students make the transition smoother. As you can imagine, everyone was in an uproar and nervous about closing our beloved school that possessed so much history. Many of our parents had attended Spaugh, so to learn our school was closing was a sobering time for everyone. In typical Barnes fashion, my friend-maintained staff and family morale, helping to make a negative situation somewhat bearable.

After the school closed, Barnes's own vision to lead a school was realized. In 2019, she became the founding principal of a middle school. She epitomized the quote "The only thing worse than being blind is having sight but no vision," and her students, families, and the community followed her unwavering leadership. I am excited to continue to see the results of her leadership come to fruition.

I ask you: What is your short- and long-term vision, and how will you make sure it comes to fruition?

# 17

*"If better is a possibility, then good is no longer an option"*

**~ Ken Griffin."**

(This quote applies to James Ford, mentee, educator, long-time friend, educational consultant, activist, and former North Carolina Teacher of the Year, 2014–2015.)

Being in the room with James Ford is like being in a room with one of the smartest and most humble men in the world. He has been in education for over fifteen years and has no plans of leaving this profession anytime soon. James has held several leadership roles in education; he will tell you he is a servant leader in all capacities. He balances work with serving as a minister, writer, activist, and educational consultant while being a devoted husband and father of four beautiful children.

His leadership style and wisdom instantly attract people, making them want to lean in and learn. His modest yet fierce actions to fight for educational justice are at the core of who he is. He asks the hard questions, such as, "Is this equitable?" "Who is benefiting from this educational system?" "Are you a value-add?" "Are there better opportunities for our black and brown children?" "Will you remain in the stands, or will you play on the court?" All of these questions that he poses align with his belief that if better is a possibility, then good is no longer an option for our children, families, educators, and community!

In our first conversation back in 2012, when I was serving as an assistant principal and he was a committed world history teacher at Garinger Senior High School, he made sure I knew that making sure students received the truth about their history was not an option! Students never missed his class because they knew they would learn, and learning is indeed what they did every day in Mr. Ford's class. I stand in sheer admiration of his knowledge about how to effectively teach students, lead conferences, and engage in conversations about racism and class. I also admire how he has never shied away from the equity issues that need to be addressed head-on. He cares deeply about our children, educators, and community.

James is an icon in the educational community at the local, state, and national levels. He will not take credit for his success but instead always credits the amazing people around him; that humility always rings true. If you don't know James Ford, he is one that I highly encourage you to research. He truly epitomizes this quote, "If better is a possibility, then good is no longer an option" for our kids, educators, and the community.

In what areas of your personal and professional life do you believe better opportunities abound?

## 18

*"Will you remain in the stands or will you get in the game?"*

**~ Dr. Christa Flood.**

(This quote applies to Jan McIver, long-time friend, former colleague, and current principal.)

Almost twenty years ago, I met Jan when I was asked by her principal to serve as a motivational speaker to a group of middle school students to encourage them to pass their end-of-grade tests. Jan was the assistant principal at the middle school. She and I conversed about how motivational words can mean the world to children, all children. Her passion and love for students resonated in our initial conversation.

Fast forward. We continued to collaborate about various projects and initiatives, and the ultimate goal we set out to accomplish was to complete Wingate University's add-on administrative license and doctoral program. In 2011, Jan was promoted to principal at Bishop Spaugh Middle School, a Title I school, and asked if I would join her as assistant principal. It was through our close working relationship that I witnessed her unwavering commitment to advocate for black and brown students. I witnessed Jan on phone calls and in meetings asking hard questions such as, "What does that decision mean for our kids who may lack resources?" and "Are parents' voices included in this decision?"

Jan fought hard, I mean, really fought hard for equitable resources for our students and has not stopped. She would often hear "no" to requests, but she didn't accept it for our students. She started partnerships with food banks, churches, and other various organizations to support our students, staff, parents, and the community. She was not just a "fan" of equity for our kids, she was active on the court and continues as of today.

She is a leader among leaders in the educational arena and will give credit to others for her accomplishments over her twenty years in education. Jan is the person who will drive to children's homes to deliver items, write proposals to seek resources for our children, attend school board meetings, question the status quo that doesn't benefit children, and speak about systematic racism. I am confident that her two young sons are proud of their mother and that they, too, will use their voices to bring about change and advocate for the rights of black and brown children.

So, I ask you, will you remain in the stands cheering others on, or will you get in the game by fighting for equity and equality for our children?

# *19*

*"[Wealth] only magnifies who you really are"*

~ **Robert Kiyosaki.**

(This quote applies to Marilyn McIntyre, long-time friend and former colleague from the Charlotte-Mecklenburg school system.)

If you want to meet the most caring, loving, and generous person in the world, you have to meet Marilyn McIntyre. She came into my life in 2004. I was a Language Arts coach for the school district, and she was an experienced teacher. I recall thinking to myself, *What feedback am I supposed to offer a veteran teacher with my limited eight years of teaching experience?* As educators who care deeply about children, fellow teachers, and the community as a whole, we began to intentionally support each other. Her natural ability to lead others made our collaboration seamless. She and I spent many days discussing best teaching practices. A year later, she would apply for a position on our Curriculum and Instruction Team, and our professional relationship went from me supporting her to us working in parallel roles. The respect and admiration we had for each other were manifested in our ability to lead others toward growth and success.

Marilyn is such a loving person, point-blank. Her unselfish ways are demonstrated through giving to others, practicing random acts of kindness, and providing food for others, all of which magnify her true character. I have seen her provide words of encouragement to a teacher who felt they were not doing enough for their kids, which empowered that teacher to do remarkable things in her classroom. Marilyn helped to fill in the financial gap for teachers by purchasing lunch for them when payday was far away. The list could go on for days, but I am here to tell you she has done multiple acts of service without looking for anything in return. Wealth is often associated with money, but in this example, wealth means random acts of kindness, which are far more valuable than any dollar amount.

How do you model your wealth in your daily actions?

# 20

*"Your attitude is like a price tag, it shows how valuable you are"*

**~ Sharath Aradnya.**

(This quote applies to Deborah Goddard, mentee and friend.)

Deborah and I met in 2014 when she joined the 2015 Teach For America corps in Charlotte, North Carolina after relocating from Maryland. In all my interactions with her, she had the most positive and uplifting attitude one could ever experience. Her smile was genuine, heartfelt, and sincere. It was natural for her to ask how she should help and support others when she was a new teacher herself. She would go on to teach scholars at West Mecklenburg High School, leading her students to achieve the highest biology test results in the school district. She never takes credit as an individual for her students' successful academic performance; she will tell you it was because of a team approach.

In speaking with anyone who knows Deborah, they will tell you her attitude and love for others resonates. She continues to volunteer in the community. I can remember on a hot Saturday morning, she met with her students in front of a black-owned restaurant to register voters. She is on the front line of fighting for educational justice for children. Eventually, she was hired on staff at Teach For America to work as a first-year teacher leadership coach. Her attitude has made the difference in leading teachers and working with colleagues. Amid the uncertainty and confusion that exists at times with leading teachers, you can rest assured that her attitude shows her value and the value of teachers. Deborah truly believes that if she can help change an outcome for even just one child, then she knows her work with teachers was worth it.

If you want to be inspired and motivated to do the work needed for our students, teachers, and the community, meet Deborah, and it will innately happen. She has truly modeled how her positive attitude has served as a price tag showing her incredible value. How much is your attitude worth?

# 21

*"Are you a bucket filler or a bucket dipper?"*

**~ Author Unknown.**

(This quote applies to Anne Marie Martin, high school teacher and former member of our Teach For America Alumni Advisory Board in Charlotte, North Carolina.)

Have you ever talked to a person multiple times, and each time you left them, you felt more inspired than ever before? They fill your spirit with positive words, affirmations, kudos, kindness, and an overall love for life. I feel this way every time I speak with Anne Marie Martin. She finds optimism in every aspect of life, whether we are discussing school-related issues, worldly topics, or personal experiences. Every person needs to find a person such as this in their life. Luckily, Anne Marie is an amazing teacher who can do this every day with students.

Keep a bucket filler in your life, and stay away from people who attempt to dip from your bucket. Those would be people who consistently speak negative words. You say it is a beautiful day and they say, "It is going to rain later." Watch the people you allow to enter your circle.

Are you a bucket filler or bucket dipper?

# 22

*"If you change nothing, nothing changes"*

**~ Joyce Brothers.**

(This quote applies to Robin Green, CMS Coordinator, former Assistant Principal for Charlotte Mecklenburg Schools, and long-time friend.)

"Visionary," "advocate," "catalyst," and "drill sergeant" is how I describe my long-time friend. Robin and I met some ten years ago, working closely as administrators at a high school in Charlotte, North Carolina. From the moment I met Robin, she was developing plans to support teachers, students, and parents and bringing the community together. Robin is the person who is unafraid to ask the hard questions about systems and structures that aren't focused on children. If systems are broken, she will fight to change them. I remember when the graduation requirements changed, she orchestrated a communication plan along with the guidance counselors. Parents were invited to the school, where she empowered both students and parents to ensure their opinions and perspectives were included in the plan.

Robin doesn't just wait for someone to make changes; she is the change agent, developing solutions in collaboration with key stakeholders. I have watched her calm academic storms. Students understand that she shows tough love because she sees the strengths in others and only wants the greatest to come out of them. She is the one who plans and leads work at her church, Greek sorority, and numerous community programming events and activities. No matter where she is working, Robin's impact spans more than twenty years. She has added value and changed the trajectory of hundreds of children and families. Robin is one who truly believes that if you change nothing, nothing changes.

What changes have you led?

# 23

*"A bend in the road is not the end of the road unless you fail to make the turn"*

**~ Helen Keller.**

(This quote applies to Tim Hurley, long-time friend and former executive director.)

Tim came into my life eight years ago when he took a chance and hired me on staff at Teach For America. We immediately bonded because of our love and passion for black and brown children. Tim welcomed my passionate and fiery communication style when advocating for students and doing right by children. His actions matched his words when he encouraged myself and others to be our authentic selves. He trusted my decisions to lead programming that provided access and opportunities to children.

Tim and his beautiful wife encountered a bend in the road when their triplets were born in 2013 with severe health complications. This was a scary time for his family and all loved ones, as they had to manage ongoing and intense medical support to keep their babies alive. I watched Tim and his family's faith increase every day as their little ones fought hard. Today, that bend in the road is no longer there, as their triplets are healthy and happy, living lives just like other children. Although one of the children faces lifelong challenges, he is thriving each day.

I then witnessed Tim experience another bend in the road when he was offered an executive director role with the Movement School, which meant he would leave Teach For America to start a new career. To be transparent, I had mixed emotions, because he was the one who had hired me in this new role as a sixteen-year educator, and now he would be transitioning into a new role. However, after several conversations, we agreed that work for children would never stop. We would just spread out our love and passion for kids in different working spaces. Today, that bend in the road has opened opportunities and access to even more children and families in the Charlotte area, and his decision was a game-changer in our community.

The respect I have for Tim is such that words can't explain. He epitomizes the idea that when a bend comes in the road, just make that turn, and it will yield positive results. When have you reached a bend in the road and decided to make a turn? What was the result?

# 24

*"Don't look back. You're not going that way"*

**~ Mary Engelbreit.**

(This quote applies to Tonya E. Askew, best friend.)

How many people can say they have had the same friend for over forty years? I am one of those people. My best friend and I have known each other since kindergarten. We grew up in Northampton County, also called "the 252" due to our area code. If you grew up in the 252, you developed a bond with your friends that has lasted a lifetime.

As I think about my best friend, I am reminded about how she wanted to be her genuine and authentic self as a child while striving to follow the expectations of her family culture. However, it wasn't easy, because she didn't want to be disrespectful towards family values. The pressure of her fitting into the school culture often created tension. Bullying in school was a norm, but we didn't know what to even call it in the late '80s. We just knew some children weren't being nice. Some of the pressures Tonya faced included not being able to wear certain clothes, including pants, as she was raised to wear only dresses and skirts, attending church multiple times a week when other kids could attend sporting events and dances, and not being allowed to date in high school. But my friend made the best choice for herself and overcame it all. Although she overcame this phase in her life, it didn't go without Tonya having a stigma or label attached to her. She was often criticized for having a "big mouth," always in the principal's office and often in fights just as a means of self-preservation. Unbeknownst to many, she was the victim but was often seen as the culprit. She will tell you she's thankful for her parents, her upbringing and foundation—they made her stronger as a person, and she instilled these values in her two children, who are adults now.

At times she has had to look back, but she quickly reminds herself that looking forward to the great things she has accomplished is her new direction. Her past enabled her to serve at-risk youth and families for well over twenty years, and in retrospect, she understands you can only advise well in areas where you have experience. Her past has also ignited her as a "change agent," as she firmly believes no one should know something is wrong, see it is wrong, and yet look the other way. She serves as a foster parent licensing supervisor and advocates for the safety and well-being of youth and families, while being a role model and using her upbringing as a springboard to encourage children to be their authentic selves at all times.

I am immensely proud of my best friend due to her ability to forward-think in all situations. Why must you look forward, even in times of uncertainty?

# 25

*"You cannot solve a problem with the same consciousness that created it"*

**~ Albert Einstein.**

(This quote applies to Katherine Bradley-Martin, long-time friend.)

"I would like to schedule a meeting to discuss a role on staff at Teach For America; when are you available?" asked Katherine. "I can meet tomorrow at 4 pm," I said. From that initial conversation in 2012, we have kept talking for eight years, and from those conversations developed our friendship. I address Katherine as "KBM," and I am thankful she has never asked me to stop!

KBM was my manager for two years on Teach For America staff, and during this time, she taught me so much about my leadership development; I am beyond grateful. This quote comes to mind with KBM because my consciousness about racial injustice was limited when we first met. I always knew something was wrong in our education system, but I lacked the skills to be able to name specific examples and identify solutions. Questioning the bias in the statewide tests or the unfair suspension policies that negatively impacted black and brown children or pushing for Diversity, Equity, and Inclusiveness training for the school district are all examples that come to mind for me now. Learning from KBM opened my eyes to how I could add even more value to the broken systems that exist in our society.

In order to solve broken systems that create and perpetuate inequality for kids, though, I first had to unpack my own consciousness, which had been developed for years. KBM and I learned together, grew together, and are better advocates for children today because we understand our own consciousness created by our backgrounds and life experiences. We challenged each other in ways that helped us each sharpen our own leadership. She as a white woman and I as a black woman developed a bond that will never be broken. KBM is an ally in racial justice and educational inequity work, which she consistently supports through paths such as scholarships to help children graduate from college, mentoring relationships with young females, and service on community boards to ensure equity is at the center of decisions. With KBM's support and encouragement, I channeled my love for others and passion for education into more specific advocacy for racial justice.

Has your own consciousness ever held you back from solving an issue? What steps can you take to change it?

# 26

*"Win if you can, lose if you must, but never quit"*

**~ Cameron Trammell.**

(This quote applies to Maurice Flood, cousin.)

My cousin Maurice brings joy, humor, and love to any space he enters. He puts everyone's needs before his own, which he will tell you brings him joy. You can find him taking care of his mother and aunt in various ways. He delivers groceries and other needed supplies to family and friends, transports folks who need transportation, and doesn't accept anything in return other than, "Thanks, Moe."

In life, you seldom find people who emulate these selfless ways, but Maurice serves as an example. I remember how he would send my mother, his Aunt Doris, the funniest cards because he knew it would bring her so much joy. He would call to hear her response; small things make a huge impact. He has been a winner with family and friends by showing unconditional love to all. He will share he has lost some special people in his life, people whom he cared so much about, but his resilience and tenacity to see the good in all life's losses have always come through. He was the one who helped the families with business affairs, a shoulder to lean on and ears to listen, without judgment, just pure concern for others. I always wondered how he was able to always be the person to stay calm in the monstrous storms of life, and he would tell anyone that he wanted to be a source of help. Throughout life's low and high days, he has lost countless times, but he has never quit. He uses his tests as a testimony to others.

When have you lost in life, but didn't quit?

# 27

*"A successful man is one who can lay a firm foundation with the bricks others have thrown at him"*

**~ David Brinkley.**

(This quote applies to Dr. Denise Watts, former Community Superintendent for Project L.I.F.T and long-time friend.)

Over twenty years ago, Dr. Watts and I began our friendship, as we taught next door to each other at a summer camp in the Grier Heights community. Anyone who knows Denise and me can tell you that we are passionate, dramatic, and boisterous to say the least. Our friendship immediately took off, and we remain friends to this very day.

Denise is one of the most intelligent, compassionate visionaries you will ever meet. She has served in a variety of leadership roles, including teacher, assistant principal, principal, and executive director, and she now does leading work for an educational company. In her role as Executive Director for Project LIFT, an initiative that sought to meet a 90/90/90 goal for seven Title I schools, she worked on one of her most challenging and rewarding projects, which I personally witnessed. She galvanized a community of educators, students, and community leaders through her servant leadership.

The community often questioned Project LIFT's ability to close the achievement gap for kids, increase graduation rates, and make an impact in the lives of children. Yet in most areas, the project succeeded. Denise navigated the negative publicity that was often highlighted in the media by continuing to lay a strong foundation even when bricks of "opposition" were thrown at her. She remained committed to her goal to help students grow academically, one day at a time and one obstacle at a time. Denise is a wife and mother, as well, who will tell you she has done work in the educational field for years not only for her children but for children in the Charlotte Mecklenburg community. Her goal has been to work toward empowering students from vulnerable communities by establishing opportunities and support that allows them to learn, grow, and be great leaders. To know Denise is to know she is a mover and shaker for kids, and no bricks will ever hold her back from doing what is right by children.

When have you continued to lay a firm foundation when bricks were thrown at you?

# 28

*"Live your life as a thank you every day!"*

### ~ Dr. Christa Flood.

(This quote applies to Aunt Dottie [Doris] Flood.)

Oh, my Aunt Dottie: She can repair a car, plant flowers, fix a leaky faucet, cook bacon, and talk on the phone all at the same time. We laugh profusely about how she is able to complete multiple tasks at one time. Everybody has that one person in the family that serves as the backbone for everyone; well, in the Flood family, it is my Aunt Dottie. She gets pleasure when she can help someone and lives her life as a "thank you" because of people who have helped her throughout life. When you engage in conversation with her, you will leave inspired and grateful for life.

She has often told stories about how my grandparents, whom I never met, valued family. I feel like I know them on a personal level because of the stories shared about them. The most memorable story was about how a cookout on Labor Day led to our family reunion tradition of forty-three years. After my grandparents passed away, Aunt Dottie vowed to keep the tradition alive.

She still resides in the house she grew up in and takes such good care of the property along with my Aunt Shirletha. Aunt Dottie has hosted our family reunion at her home for over forty years by preparing the landscape, making sure the children have games, and doing tons of logistical things to be ready for close to 300 people. This is not an easy task, but she will tell you she is thankful to be able to organize it each year and that joy comes when she sees our family fellowshipping together. I have never heard her complain about anything other than to say we need "more" of something to help another person. Her humbleness and kindness are examples of how people should be in the world. Did I also tell you if you want to hear a good joke, she is the one to talk with? You will leave with your side hurting.

Who is the backbone in your family? Do you, too, live your life as a thank you because of someone?

# 29

*"If you don't like something, just take away its only POWER: Your attention"*

**~ Author Unknown.**

(This quote applies to Amanda Thompson, mentee, former colleague, and long-time friend.)

"I am Amanda Thompson, and I need to talk to you, Ms. Flood, about something personal."

I remember this conversation like it was yesterday. Thompson was a new teacher, and I was a new assistant principal at the school. I immediately told her we could talk, and she revealed that she was having her first child. I was elated for her! However, she was nervous about being a new mom while balancing work responsibilities. We came up with a plan, and close to nine years later, Addison is a smart and beautiful young lady, and Thompson is an amazing teacher leader, mother, and advocate for children. She and I often reminisce about this conversation and how her life is a model for others.

During that same year, we discussed how her advocacy platform could change the trajectory for hundreds of scholars, because all she wanted were the same opportunities for black and brown kids that more affluent kids were privileged to have. She was a visionary, seeing her daughter's future along with those of other children. Now, ten years later, Thompson's name is always used in the same sentence as "advocate." If she doesn't like the way certain things are affecting kids and her community, such as political issues, opportunities and access for kids, teacher pay, and so on, she will fight until the end. She has decided that her attention will only be focused on issues that bring fairness and equity to others. You will see Thompson on the news, in newspapers, on social media, at rallies, and in other spaces advocating for others. She is the "go-to person" to get results. She's intentional about who and what she gives her attention to and has been a model for so many people, especially in the educational and political arena. I have often told her, "You are the real MVP" while thanking her for using her voice to bring about change.

What will you give your attention to that really matters?

# *30*

*"DNA doesn't equal family. Love does"*

**~ Author Unknown.**

(This quote applies to "Def Row," my line sisters whom I pledged with in 1994 and long-time friends.)

One would assume that by definition alone, the words "DNA" and "love" are synonymous. If that has been your belief system, then this next quote about twenty-one sisters who were not connected by DNA will surely dispel that line of thinking.

On April 20, 1994, I officially became a member of the renowned Delta Sigma Theta Sorority, Inc. (DST) with twenty other beautiful and soulful Black women. Like the twenty-two sisters who founded DST, our bond grew out of purpose, a commitment to serve, and loyalty to one another. There was nothing too hard for "Def Row" as we boldly engaged in community activities, random acts of kindness, quality time, and even some mischievousness together. We were malleable young women who had no shortage of fun, learning to step and competing against other Greek organizations. The relationships and memories made as we matriculated through the pledge process were priceless, and the memories are forever with me. The love I have for my twenty line sisters has strengthened over the last twenty-six years. All those experiences, old and new, made us sisters, even though we were not connected by DNA.

Now in our forties and fifties, the core of what made us "Def Row" still exists. We continue to connect, call, check in, serve, support, and leverage one another for advice, which continues to reinforce our bond. I am indebted to Delta Sigma Theta Sorority, Inc. for allowing me the opportunity to gain twenty sisters whom I will always LOVE although we don't share the same DNA.

Who do you consider a sister or brother although they may not be biologically related to you?

# Acknowledgments

I want to give thanks and praise to my Lord and Savior, Jesus Christ. I want to thank you for giving me the discipline, insight, and tenacity to write my first book. Without you, I am nothing.

Thank you to my family, friends, Delta Sigma Theta line sisters, colleagues at Teach For America-Charlotte Region, and every person highlighted in this book for brainstorming with me and consistently pushing me to complete the book. Thank you to my siblings for being there for me and planting positive seeds in my life: Deon Flood, Linda Hardy, Zelma Williams, and Debra Denson.

Specifically, I want to thank Moni Ward, Lakecia Neal, Tonya Askew, Starlet Deloatch, Maurice Flood, Dr. Chena Flood, Keon Artis, Tomiaka Wingard, Kendra Alston, Philana Woods, Lakisha Grant, Mariam Tisdale, Caitlin Collins, Kyra Jackson, Ceriese Blue, and Deborah Goddard for the countless recommendations, ideas, thoughts, and words of encouragement. Every time I asked a question, you all were there to respond and push me forward.

Your words of encouragement are the reason why the book is finally completed. If you don't have people in life who are your supporters and who believe in you, you may want to change your circle. I am blessed that I have all of you in my circle. I am indebted to you for all your love and support throughout the process of completing my first book.